FALLING IN LOVE WITH POETRY

DAKIARA

MIND FLOW PUBLISHING & PRODUCTION LLC PRESENTS

Falling in Love With Poetry

DaKiara

First Printing: 2020

ISBN 978-1-951271-10-7 Paperback

ISBN 978-1-951271-11-4 Ebook

Additional copies of this book and others are available by mail or by visiting the website listed below. Check website for pricing.

Mind Flow Publishing & Production LLC PO Box 48768 Cumberland, North Carolina 28331-8768 www.mindflowpublishingproduction.com

Cover design by Carrie & Co.

Editing by Stories Matter Editing

Typesetting Design by Chy Illustrations

Formatting by Covers My Way

Thank you for helping to bring Mary B to Life......

DEDICATION

DEDICATED TO MY LOVES

DAQUAN, DEJA, DANTE
KEVONN AND KIARA

RIP
DAQUAN JAMIQUE 95
KIARA DENISE 00

Special Thanks to GOD for Giving Me the Strength and the
Words to Do This Project. Blessed by The Experiences to
Draw From
It Has Not Always Been Easy.

Dedicated to Some Who Have Gone Before Me Mary Merriman
Naomi Thompson

Falling in Love with Poetry

Poetry is the music of the soul
Listen carefully as the stories unfold
When your favorite singer sings
From deep inside the lyrics bring
Forth emotions and desires
Designed to inspire
Generations to come
The love affair has begun
Nikki Giovanni is one of the greats
In my opinion to date
Her lyrics moved me
Made it quite clear to see
This is where my heart was meant to be
When writing my words
Speaking my truths
I am at peace
Simply from sharing with you
A piece of my soul

Thinking of Love

When I think of love
I don't think about the flowers
Or the candy and other gifts
That I've been showered with for years
I think of the fact
That with you I'm safe and secure
And you've somehow erased
My deepest fears
I think about the many times
I've cried
And all my tears
You've dried
When I think of love
I simply think of you

Soul Mate

How is it that after many years
You still send shivers
Throughout my soul
I used to kid myself
Acting as if
I had control
The reality is clear to see
Our love
Was meant to be
I get all giggly inside
These feelings too strong
And never to be denied
Just one quick question
What would it take
For you to be my bride

Being in Love

Is one of the most
Euphoric feelings in this world
Some are only lucky to feel this once
In a lifetime
What happens
When it happens
Repeatedly
Is that really love
Or just a vicious cycle
Destined to repeat
Or is it a second chance
At love
How sweet

The First Time

My first experience with this
Was through song
I made the connection
As I let the rhythm fill me
As I happily sang along
I then took pen to paper
And began
My own journey
Into the rapper's delight
Using my words
My battles to fight
This is where
My first love
Took flight

Two Hearts

Two hearts that beat as one
How is this possible?
Of this love, what is to become?
Can the two coexist?
Bringing about new twists
Familiar, yet new
Exciting, yet true
The hearts have found their rhythm
Beating in perfect timing
This love, forever binding
Two hearts begin anew

Battle with My Pen

This page is taunting me
The words wont appear
When they do
Will they release my deepest fear
Or tell of enlightenment
Or of yesterdays excitement
This fight is daily
I'm determined to win
As the day breaks
The battle with my pen
Is destined to begin

Your Eyes

They say, eyes are the windows to the soul
What if that is a lie we were told
What if they were simply a thing of beauty to behold
Your eyes remind me of chocolate truffles
Decadent and rich
Taking a bite
True bliss
I'm helpless as your eyes draw me in
Again and again
If your eyes held the secrets within
Would you
Let me in

Perfect Match

My mental has been shook
From you
With only one look
Well maybe two
Didn't take long
To know I was through
You are the missing link
The one who makes me think
You've opened my heart
It's hard to picture
Us apart
A perfect match
We fuss
We love
We conquer all

Show & Tell

You asked me once to be yours
To this I agreed
It was your smooth touch
Gentle kisses
Sultry voice
As you whispered my name
The shallow breaths
As your body
I claimed
You asked me to be yours
Your body showed me that and more

Desire

Where did you come from?
How did you ease into and overtake my mind?
For years, I've maintained my walls.
With a few breaths
They crumbled
Ceased to exist
There is only you
You became the walls around my heart
My soul is yours to protect
Where do we start....

I Love You

Three words contain so much power
When combined with actions
Leaves nothing to be desired
When you say I love you
It sends a tingle up my spine
Often makes me rewind
Thoughts of yesterday
That's where I find
Thoughts of you
Your actions support your words
I love you

Queen

My love for you
Daily it grows
Its presence shows
In all that I do
Day after day
I still choose you
My body aches for your touch
Words can never
Express how much
You truly mean
You are my world
My one true Queen

The Future

Who knew when we met
That our best was yet
To come
Our friendship blossomed
I think it's quite awesome
To have a friend for life
To help with the strife
We encounter
You're there when I need
A kind word or two
I'll always be there
To see you through

Real Friend

Friends like you are hard to find
Glad to know that you are mine
You've offered a shoulder in which to lean
A positive word, when in need
As the years go past
No worries, this will last
Our bond is too strong to break
A bond like this can't be fake
Blessed to call you my friend
I'd choose you again

My Superhero

Super heroes don't always wear capes
But, their shoes no one can mistake
You see
Aunt Bay Bay you are classy
You make us all glad to be
In your presence
Basking in your essence
You have always pushed
Me towards my destiny
Never once second guessed me
Showed me it's okay to be free
You are humble
With so much style
You've been my inspiration
For quite a while
I've watched how you navigate life
Even from afar
You taught me how to be a good wife
So for you
This is my dedication

Aunt Bay Bay the world is yours
You've taught me it's okay to explore
Nothing wrong with wanting more
On this day
I simply wanted to say
You are my Superhero
One that isn't afraid to rock her stilettos
Unconditional Love
Is your Super Power

Precious Moments

In a moment
Your life can flash before your eyes
Because of this fact
Always think before you act
Greet your loved ones with a smile
One never knows
When their card will be punched
Call your mom
Share a lunch
An hour of your time
Not one single dime
Was spent
Precious memories
Instead
Take a moment
To smell the daisies
Never second guess
And think maybe
You could be doing
Something different

Tick Tock

What if 60 seconds was all you had
To show your love
Your love
How would you proceed
Would you complete
The deed
Or would you leave them starved
Only after setting
The bar
Would you pull them in
Embrace from within
Your heart will win

Momma

Words won't ever express
The way my heart feels
Distressed
I know in time the pain will ease
I'm sitting here
Smiling through the pain
Underneath
My heart has never known
Such pain
Without words you always knew
Who will I go to
To get me through
I know I have to let you go
There is something
I need you to know
You will never be forgotten
We will never let it happen
You've touch so many
Those who love you

Plenty
Rest easy

Just Breath

Watching you from afar
You are oblivious to me
I see the sway of your hips
Nah love, don't even trip
I'm not on that stalker tip
You are one fine honey dip
If only you could see
How right I am for you
Not like those other dudes
Who simply use and abuse
With me you can be happy
Not to get all sappy
I'm a man you see
I'm strong and hard
The way a man is supposed to be
Until you breath
Captivating me
Suddenly afar isn't far at all

Hello

Excuse me
May I have a word with you
I've noticed you for quite some time
Had to work my nerve up to step to you
I realize I had to come correct
I am too afraid that you will reject
My sincerest advances
Therefore lessening my chances
Of getting to know you
So humbly I say
Hello, can I get to know you

Past Thoughts

Thinking about my past
I have to laugh
My smile
Hides the pain
Just as others have
I survived the storming rain
My life was threatened
A time or two
One of my secrets
Not many knew
It's hard to let people inside
So much easier for me to hide
The hurt and the pain
Some brought me shame
As time went on
I realized
I was no longer alone
You helped me open up
Told me it was ok to not give up
In my darkest times

You never let up
You showed me strength
I never knew I had
Thinking back
At times
I become sad
At the wasted time
The past I can't change
Thanks to you
My future has been rearranged

Real Talk

Since you've been gone
My heart beat is off track
My mind is in a state of confusion
Closing my eyes, I'm hoping it's an illusion
Sadly the conclusion
I simply want you back
You may think I'm joking
I assure you it's true

The Score

Starring at the walls
My mind is in a frenzy
My mental is on overload
Thoughts disorganized
Running rampant
They won't let me sleep
Yet the words
My mouth won't speak
I try to coax them out
Swipe them like a bandit
Waiting on their next score

Your Smile

From the moment, I laid my eyes on you
I felt myself melt into your pretty browns
You looked deep into my core
Whispered sweet somethings to my soul
Your scent teased my senses
As I begged for more
Your love was made just for me
We fit like that snug glove
On a cold winter's night
I bask in the radiance from your smile
You make living
Worthwhile

Sincerely

I saw the look in your eyes
It hurt me
Sadden me
To know I'm the reason why
I didn't mean it
When I said goodbye
This was never meant to last
There were to many secrets
Skeletons in our past
You made me forget
All the hurt I knew
That came with loving you
Your caring nature
Unselfish ways
Brought the sun
Into my gloomy days
My heart and soul
Is yours
It's true
I just can't go on

Living with you
We love
We fight
Just couldn't get it right
I will always love you
Know that my feelings are
Sincerely true

Let's Play

My words
Are like katana's
They cut deep
Death by
A million cuts
Yeah
That's deep
Can you survive
The assault
On your mental
Listen carefully
As the instrumental
Of your life
Begins to play
Hold tight
As I begin
To slay

Mental Trip

May I take a trip
Through your mind
What kind of secrets
Are there for me to find
Would I learn what makes you tick
How about what excites you
Listen a moment
As I enlighten you
When I touch
Your inner thoughts
You begin to lick your lips
At that moment
I begin to drip
Be careful now
The stick of dynamite
Has been lit
As I stroke
The intimate corners
Of your mind
Ecstasy is what you will find

Your mind
My mind
Simultaneously
Combust
I can feel the thrust
As your soul
Devours mine
May I
Take that trip
Around your mind

Changes

I see you butterfly
Would you fly for me
Spread your wings
And glide for me
Would you give up
Your freedom
To stay with me
I've watch you
Flourish and grow
From a plain cocoon
I've watched you bloom
Your colors are etched
Within my mind
You were my treasure
To find
Would you
Could you
Be mine..

Chameleon

In the distance
An alarm is sounding
Reminding me
That within me
There is a fire burning
Strong and fierce
At first glance
I seem
Meek
Humble
Calm
Collected
But inside
My mind
Thoughts of
A sinister kind
As thoughts
Make their way
To my tongue
Watch out

It burns
Not to be taken lightly
When my thoughts
Are unleashed
Upon this world
It's enough
To make your
Essence shake
That's something
Hard to fake...
Real tough
To emulate

Plaything

I'm watching you
As you watch me
Your body movements
Excite me
You play coy
Yet offering
Yourself up to me
As my toy
This is something
I truly enjoy
For now
I get to play
And have things
My way
Your gentle kiss
Takes me on a journey
To perfect bliss

You

You ask, why you
I say, why not you
You are the yang
To my ying
It's for you
And only you
That my heart sings
From time to time
I feel the flutters
I admit
You even
Make me stumble
Over my words
As I try to impress you
All the while
My eyes undress you
You are the calm
To my storm
It's for you

That my heart bleeds
It's you
That fulfill my needs

Snake Bite

I hear you
Before I feel you
You are so sleek
Gentle and meek
Most fear your bite
But for me
You're just right
On my worst days
Your curious ways
Comfort me
In ways
Others have yet to understand
With you there is just me
If only others could see
You are my gentle beast
And I
Your Reptilian Queen

Head Held High

Today is the day
That I take my life back
I've been beat down
Talked about
To where I began
To doubt myself
And question my worth
My rightful place
In this world
That I tried so hard
To conform too
For so long
I worried how others felt
That I forgot
To pay attention
To how I felt
Today I realize
My life matters
Today I reclaim

My rightful place
Upon my throne

Who am I

Who am I
I've been often asked
I am a powerful being
Who has birthed millions
Babies
Thoughts
Ideas that have
Affected the masses
I've been the anchor
To many things
Am I credited
Not in the traditional way
I've been
Raped
Assaulted
And still I stand
My spirit they've tried to break
But it simply
Wasn't theirs to take
So you ask

Who am I
I am everything
I am apart of all
That is...
I am every woman

Stay Woke

Stay Woke
They chant
While others take it for a joke
Stay woke
They chant
While others remain confused
Stay woke
They chant
To make an appearance on the news
Stay woke
They chant
While so many die
Stay woke
They chant
While blood is shed
Stay woke
They chant
As our children are raised by each other
Stay woke
They chant

Lessons

Sitting here
Alone with my thoughts
Thinking over
The mistakes I've made
Some of them
I'd do again
Just to see
If finally,
I would win
The outcomes
Remain unchanged
But a lesson learnt

Sensual

Have you ever
Smelled a smell
That reminded you of me
If not
Then my goal
Is to climb inside your mental
And engage your thoughts
In some mental foreplay
Would you allow me to have my way
I promise if you do
Ohhh the thoughts
Of me and you
I want to be intimate
With your thoughts
I want to know
What makes you tick
Isn't that some ish
I need to know
That I can stimulate
Your very soul

That means
I need to know
You beyond the physical
Into the astrophysical
Yeah I'm on some deep ish
I want our thoughts
To intertwine
Tell me you
You don't mind
Just thinking about it
Divine

Lovely Goodbyes

A million tears
Have been shed
Since our good byes
Were said
I thought
It was for the best
So now I'm here
Relieving the pain
From my chest
I never knew
Moving on could hurt
This much
Yet I still crave
Your touch
Our goodbyes
Were said
They were needed
Before someone
One of us
Wound up dead

We loved hard
We fought hard
The love went beyond
The physical
We entered
The mental realm
That is when
We finally took

Back the Healm

Of our lives
We woke up
Finally heard
Each other's cry
The love we shared
Couldn't be denied
The sound
Of goodbye
Was much sweeter
Although we may be
A little bitter....

Pain

Literally I'm petrified
Contemplating suicide
How do you kill
What's inside
In my heart
Is where it resides
The pain
Only intensifies
Gradually
I will rise

Lupus, You Disgust Me

Why did you choose me
I don't want to be
The poster child for you
A disease
Upon my body you feed
Hard for me to believe
I was so vibrant and such
Most days, you are too much
I can't let you win
So each day
A new fight begins
Although my joints may ache
My happiness
You will never take
Always until the end
My life I will defend
Relinquish your hold
You've been told
My body no longer

Yours to adorn
Take heed
Shots fired
You've been warned

When She Calls

When she calls
I dare not disregard
She is etched
Deep within the walls
Of my mind
The overwhelming need
To fulfill her every wish
It must be a sign
That she and I are destined
And the journey we must take
Isn't one
To be questioned
As her words are released
Sometimes they hurt
But in the end
All are pleased
Her one true desire
Is only to inspire
By simply
Lighting the fire

That sparks your mind
When she calls
Be prepared
Giving into her
Is simply a must

Chasing the Dragon

As my eyes close
I'm taken to a place
I used to know
One where it's no longer safe to go
Along that path a lot of death
People who have given their wealth
Giving their last breath
Just for a taste of release
There is no more caging the beast
Once she's been released
She wreaks havoc and chaos
Many lives lost
Chasing a feeling
Too many willing
Craving the thrill
No longer is this my fate
No longer is she my date
My sleep turns peaceful
Once more

Man, of Mine

You are the glue that hold us together
Countless times you've gone above and beyond to ensure
We as a family are good
Your selfless actions make me love you more
You are the man I forever will adore
If I could, I would give you the world
My heart is forever yours
We have a lifetime to explore
My greatest moments have been with you
Love you today and forever more

Hey Girl

Hey girl
Come here
Let me vibe with you
Would you allow me to take a ride with you
What if I wanted to wine and dine with you
At the end of the night
Can you ride with me
Allow me to slide

You Chose Me

Watching you from afar
Wondering just how far
I would go to keep your heart
I'm not sure how to start
I've never been scared of love
That is until, I found you
Your love has pulled me through
A desperate time or two
Who honestly knew
When I first met you
That you would love me too

Joyful Times

The holidays are here
World filled with cheer
For a few days
We put aside our hateful ways
Choosing to show love and care
To everyone everywhere
If only this was our reality
A beautiful world this would be
Instead the hate ensues
Bringing with it the blues
Loved ones lost
A terrible cost
This holiday season
Let Jesus once again be the reason
For spreading love and cheer
Throughout the whole year

Love Stopped

Interrupting my sleep
I feel you creep
Into my bed
Smelling like Chanel #5
Instead of sexing
Inquisition ahead
Who is she
Why is she between us
It's always better
When it's just us
You didn't try and hide it
Choosing to flaunt your sin
Neither of us will win
Why didn't we talk
Before it began
I know I failed
Didn't uphold my part
You dropped no hints
From the start
My broken heart

Painful Strides

Just one drink
Is all it takes
With each sip
My heart breaks
You promised you'd quit
Each time same thing
It was me you hit
Then comes the shiny new thing
Hurt feelings it can't replace
The steps can't be retraced
As the night ends
A new day begins
Bringing with it just one
My heart is done

Just Say No

I see you spiraling
Out of control
As each word
You continue to slur
Each time you promise
Never again
I sit back and wait
It happens again
This time would be different
You said you'd ease up
Possibly slow up
When the drinks are passed
Shocker
You didn't pass
And now we are here
The worst I fear
Your liver is done
The bottle won

The One

Not sure how it started
Was surprised as my lips parted
To speak the words
No one has heard
Your smile pulled me in
I felt the love within
In the end
Will love win
Two hearts become one
Never to be undone
My soul at ease
I'm ready to please
I know now
You are the one

My Crown

Long
Short
Curly
Straight
I'm always up
For a good debate
Natural hair
Is a thing of beauty
It's your crown
Wear it proud
Those afro puffs
They can't get enough
Curly locs
Please don't stop
Short fades
To long tresses
That's the way
To keep them guessing
Whatever your style
Wear it with a smile

Your hair is unique
Don't let them
Force you to think
Perm your hair on a whim
Just to satisfy them

Without You

From the moment
Out eyes connected
I knew we were destined
To walk this planet
Hand in hand
But life interjected
There was another plan
One in which
We almost crumbled
I admit the ball
I often fumbled
I allowed you to slip away
When all I really
Had to do was say
How I truly felt
My pride wouldn't allow it
Now I'm here
Without you
Happy?
Not one bit

Tia

Tia was a young girl
Who simply wanted to see the world
She had dreams of going afar
Sadly her life never got that far
In a distance he stood
No one believing he would
Take an innocent life
Because he was mad with his wife
She cheated
Tia, he greeted
If only she had run
The deed, never done
Instead she chose to smile
Making him pause for a while
Second guessing his plan
If only he would have ran
Her life would have been spared
This tale, no need to be shared

My Peace

1 9 years have gone past
Just yesterday, I thought of you last
Without warning I lost a piece of me
The hurt and pain anyone can see
You were made in my image
My very own mini me
The journey without you not easy
Please believe me
You left a part of you here
In one who I hold dear
Your brother's light truly shines
I know it's just you in disguise
As the tears begin to roll
As your loss continues its toll
I know you're at peace
So that is my peace

The Proposal

You and I together
What could be better
You've wiped my tears
And quieted my storms
You've rubbed my feet
Kissed me till I was weak
Your love you've shown
My mind, you've blown
With you is where I belong
Your own private song
It's for you I sing
Please accept my ring

Unreal

Sitting here beside you
It almost feels unreal
Your presence missed
Your kisses surreal
Without you
A part of me lost
Being without
A terrible cost
One time
I wish no longer to visit

My Prize

Stolen glance
Hoping not to miss my chance
Looking at you now
Thinking to myself how
Did I become so blessed
Just last year, stressed
You are my calm
Tracing the lines in your palm
We are meant to be
Plain to see
Seeing you with new eyes
No games, no lies
No need to bother with goodbyes
You, my love
The true prize

Finally

As my mind fills with thoughts of you
I find it hard to catch my breath
Your love is like gasoline to a fire
I'm drawn to you like a moth is to the flame
You know my every desire
No words need to be spoken
I am consumed with you
Drinking in your essence as if it were the water in my glass
Your mine
At long last

The Next

As I lay here and close my eyes
I feel your warmth
I feel your touch
And in my belly
The butterflies take flight
With each breath I take
I am overwhelmed with anticipation
Of our next....
Next hug
Next kiss
Next chat
Next smile
Next breath
Anticipation

DaQuan

Even as the years
Come and go
It doesn't stop my tears
And their constant flow
18 years have come and passed
Will I find peace at long last
Broken images flash in my mind
To a place in time
I wish to rewind
I remember your laugh
Your cry
Never did I think you would die
When you left a piece of my heart
You took
An achy feeling
That's yet to be shook

Constant

Although days may come and go
The one thing you should know
Is my love being constant and unchanging
No matter what the day may bring
For you
My heart still sings
Even when your days are long
Or you feel
Like the world did you wrong
Grab a hold of my hand
Because by your side
Is where I stand
I am constant
Unchanging

The Nightmare

A new mother's worst nightmare is born
With the birth and loss of her newborn son
These two climatic events
Occurred to close to prevent
What moments should have been happy ones
Were too quickly interrupted by unfortunate ones
Before she had time
Her gift to receive
All too quickly
The time to grieve
Was now at hand

For You

Even through the distance
Your smile brightens my day
Love it when you call
Just to say "Hey"
Hate it when you are sad and blue
My heart aches for you
Over the years
You've been there more than a time or two
Having you in my world
Helped get me through
Some rough times
That have now been left behind
Wishing that gift
I could give to you
Always know
Without a doubt
I love you

Missing You

Last night
I missed your presence
Missed feeling your arms
Wrapped around me
Keeping me safe
Throughout the night
I missed your gentle kisses
You know
The ones that warms my soul
The ones where
I feel it deep down to my toes
I missed looking into your eyes
As I drift off to sleep
And right on cue
You appear within my dreams
Last night
I missed you

The Reason

My heart has been broken
My feelings have been crushed
But none of that matters
When I look at you
Then you look at me
I feel as if I can do anything
Be anything I choose to be
The gleam in your eyes
Empower me
And the beauty of it all
Is that I know the reason you smile
Is simply for me

I'm Ready

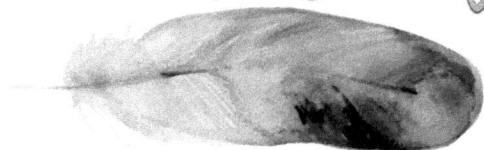

My mind unfocused
Heartbeat unsteadies
The words flow easily
Guessing now, I'm ready
To share my story
Always giving God the Glory
Heartbeat steady
My words are my weapons
I'm armed and dangerous
Please tell me, you are ready

My Time

A smile creeps upon my face
As I find myself in this well-known place
As my cheeks inflate big and wide
The excitement too strong to hide
Here I am content and willing
Excitement too much
Bouncing off the ceiling
Closing my eyes
To calm my nerves
Happiness, I too deserve

Purple Delight

If asked my color of choice
Purple represents me
Strength and pride
Yet allows my mind
To run
Wild
And free
Filled with my imagination
Hopes and dreams
Wealth and wisdom
Mine to obtain
From the spiritual
To the literal plane
Royalty by birth
Much to my delight
All things obtainable
Within my sight

THANK YOU FOR READING....

Don't forget to sign up for
Mind Flow Publishing & Production LLC's Newsletter @
www.mindflowpublishingproduction.com

Email us for autographed or additional paperback copies @
mindflowpubpro@gmail.com

OTHER TITLES ALSO AVAILABLE INCLUDE

Mental Interlude – Poetry

The Mary B Chronicles 1-4 – Fiction

Journey to Living (Kindle only) – Inspirational

Simple Complexity – Poetry

Spoken from The Heart – Poetry

Dreams Do Come True – Fiction

Charisma's Homecoming – Cozy Romance

For Her Love – Cozy Romance

Available Through

Amazon

Barnes & Noble

Kindle

Coming Soon

Freedom in the Cage Series – Fiction

A Love for Holly – Cozy Romance

A Prince for Me – Romantic Comedy

Upcoming Titles Will Be Available

Through

Amazon

Barnes & Noble

Kindle

Apple iBooks
Kobo

AUTHOR'S BIO

Although I'm still considered new to the publishing world, I have hit the ground running full speed ahead. In my first year, I was signed to Mind Flow Publishing & Production LLC, and I have published a total of 12 books. I have earned Amazon's Best Sellers Top 100 orange banner. My works are spread across several genres such as; poetry, inspirational, cozy romance, romantic comedies and Christian fiction. I will be trying my hand at cozy mysteries, romance, and sci-fi. My love for writing started when I was about 12, writing poetry and writing speeches for various oratorical contests. Inspiration for my craft is pulled from my own life experiences, as well as others. I have been featured on several podcasts, as well as Up and Coming Authors Newsletters. When I'm not writing, I love to design shadowboxes, and create personalized greeting cards. I have released my 3rd poetry book (Spoken from the Heart) in August 2019. This project is my 4th poetry release. Current books available are The Mary B Chronicles 1 - 4, Mental Interlude, and Journey to Living, Simple Complexity, and Dreams Do Come True, For Her Love, and Charisma's Homecoming. All of which are available on Amazon, and www.mindflowpublishingproduction.com.